OLD NEW ENGLAND
DOORWAYS

OLD NEW ENGLAND DOORWAYS

BY
ALBERT G. ROBINSON

WITH MANY ILLUSTRATIONS
FROM THE AUTHOR'S UNIQUE COLLECTION OF PHOTOGRAPHS OF
OLD-TIME NEW ENGLAND HOUSES AND DOORWAYS

NEW YORK
CHARLES SCRIBNER'S SONS
1919

THE SCRIBNER PRESS

DOORWAYS

DOORWAYS

HUNTING for old doorways is a harmless and interesting amusement, much like botanizing or collecting postage stamps. In addition to that, there is "the joy of the road" whether one travels afoot, in carriage, or in automobile. In New England particularly, many interesting doorways are to be found quite away from the main highways of travel, on the side streets of villages through which automobilists rush with the apparent purpose of getting somewhere rather than of seeing something, or on the little-used side roads in the country where an automobile is still a device of some wonder and even of alarm. City doorways and those in the villages may be found easily enough by inquiry or by strolling about the streets. The more isolated, the farmhouses in the country, are much less readily discovered and they sometimes come as quite delightful surprises.

Old doorways are, usually, most abundant in the old villages that have, in recent years, grown

into large towns or small cities, like Warren, in
Rhode Island, or Guilford, in Connecticut. The
latter claims more than a hundred houses built before the Revolution. But the very growth of such
places tends toward change in the old buildings.
They are modernized, or they become real-estate
derelicts or, not infrequently, tenement-houses
rapidly falling into disrepair and soon to be torn
down to make room for more profitable investments.
Naturally, the most fruitful fields are the areas of
earliest settlement, the Massachusetts shore, the
bay of Rhode Island, the towns along the Connecticut shore, and along the Connecticut River valley
as far north as Greenfield. Few of the early houses
remain in the larger cities. Most of the people of
the first century of settlement built in village groups
or not far apart along the main street. The system
had its origin in the danger from attack by Indians.
Usually, the town centre was the village green, or
common, a tract of varying area held for the common use of all for the pasturage of their cattle. A
straying cow was easily killed by a marauding
Indian, and so was a cow-owner searching afield
for his wandering beast. If a town was raided, the
compactness of its settlement made possible a

[4]

prompt concentration of the inhabitants for its defense. So they built their houses around or near the common where also were the church and the schoolhouse and, usually, a stoutly built watch-house in which the men and their families could seek refuge, and from which the plan of defense could be carried out.

As the danger from Indian attack lessened, notably after King Philip's war in 1675 and 1676, many of the colonists built their little houses on the lands bought by them or allotted to them, on the outskirts of the settlement and even farther afield. Some of the more venturesome went several miles away. Some of these early buildings were mere "dug-outs" and more were log cabins. They served their purpose for the time, but all of the "dug-outs" and cabins are now gone. Some of the settlers paid a heavy penalty for their adventure in pioneering, as did the people in Deerfield, which was destroyed by a raid from Canada, in 1704, in spite of its concentration and its protecting blockhouse. Losses by individual pioneers were numerous but few records are left to tell the story. But, with the coming of greater safety, the towns expanded, and the settler's frame house might be built a mile or

more from the village. As a general rule, it may
be set down that the greater the modern growth
of the old settlements the fewer will be the old houses
within their borders. Many of them have been
commercialized out of existence, and rows or solid
blocks of stores or shops stand where stood the ancient dwellings. Not a few still remain, modernized
out of all recognition. This is perhaps most notice-
ably shown in the towns along the Connecticut shore,
such as Fairfield, Stratford, Milford, Branford,
Guilford, and the rest. The same condition appears
in most of the old Connecticut valley towns, and
in the suburbs of Boston. Each passing year marks
the end of an appreciable number of these old buildings. Here and there, an old house is bought by
the State, or by some Historical Society, and held
as a memorial of the early days. The pity of it is
the great difficulty with which funds are raised for
this highly commendable purpose.

The particularly interesting fact about the doorways of these old dwellings is that the same designs
are found all along the Atlantic coast, from Maine
to South Carolina. This, of course, argues some
common origin for the designs. Using the term in
its modern sense, there were no professional archi-

[6]

tects in America in the seventeenth century, and few who may properly be classed as professionals in the first half of the eighteenth. In fact, most of the best work in architectural designing prior to the Revolution was done by men who may be regarded as amateurs, using the word as meaning those who cultivated and studied an art without practising it professionally. Among the amateur designers of the eighteenth century were George Washington and Thomas Jefferson; the physicians, Kearsley and Thornton and Bulfinch; Andrew Hamilton, the lawyer; Joseph Brown, the retired merchant; and Smibert, the portrait-painter.

If there is, in New England, an ornamental doorway that can, with any certainty, be assigned to the seventeenth century, it has escaped my notice. It is at least probable that such doorways were used in some of the larger and more costly city houses of that period, but I know of no such house still standing. Here and there a more or less ornate entrance appears on a house credibly claimed as of seventeenth century construction, but such are, quite certainly, an addition of a later time. There are several survivals of the early years of the eighteenth century, among them the Parson

Williams house (1707) in Deerfield, the Porter house (1713) in Hadley, and the Dummer house (1715) in Byfield. It is impossible to speak positively regarding old doorways. Some and perhaps many of them were added long after the house itself was built. As such doorways became fashionable, ornamental designs were substituted for the originals. This is sometimes determinable by the design or by the quality of the workmanship. Thus, the older part of the Samson-Frary house, in Deerfield, appears to have been built in the later years of the seventeenth century, but its porched doorway certainly was not. House and ornamental doorway were not always of contemporary construction. While there were a few exceptions, the era of decorative doorways may be regarded as beginning with what is known as the Georgian period, the date of which, in the colonies, may be given as about 1720. The doorways of houses built after that year may generally be assumed to be contemporaneous with the building.

Practically all of the houses of the seventeenth century, and most of the country houses of the greater part of the eighteenth century, were the design and workmanship of local carpenters. They were, generally, a persistence of the English type modified by local ingenuity to meet the conditions of the new country. The matter of the ornamented and ornamental doorways stands in somewhat different case. As already stated, the correspondence of designs in all of the States east of the Alleghanies, from Maine to South Carolina, argues a common origin. This is found in books on carpentry, published in England, notably, perhaps, those of which Batty Langley was the author. His books appeared at various times from 1726 to 1756. They were intended for the use of carpenters, and gave measured drawings of columns and pilasters, entablatures and architraves. From Langley and others, selections were made by the local builders who might follow the drawing with exactness, or might modify or vary the design to suit their own taste and judgment. Most of these men were masters of their craft and, moreover, were men of artistic sense. They knew the importance of proportions, and their work shows their close attention to that feature, vital in all good architecture. The leading architects of the present time can produce nothing, in doorways, superior to many of those produced by the master-artisans of the eighteenth century, and few give to the matter of proportions the careful attention that was given by the carpenter-builders of the seventeenth and the eighteenth centuries.

While stone of different kinds, and clay for brick-making, were found in endless abundance in New England, the timber-supply was no less ample. The settlers in that region had been accustomed to timber-framed houses in the land from which they came. Moreover, the wood of the country was more easily and readily worked than stone or brick. In many of the decorative doorways there is seen the result of a translation of the stone doorways of England and Europe into wood in this country. In the older lands, a stone column or pilaster supported a stone entablature or a pediment. Here, the designs of those portals were repeated or imitated in wood. In many of the entablatures and arches of wooden doorways in New England there appears a design of a central block that corresponds to the keystone of the stone portal copied or imitated. So in the wooden columns and pilasters we have the Corinthian, the Ionic and the Doric capitals. While some of the earlier work of this kind is somewhat over-heavy in design and a little rough in workmanship, it is seldom if ever offensive or objectionable to even a keen artistic sense. While the work might have been open to criticism when it was new, time has touched it with a softening hand, and some of the oldest doorways are among the most charming.

Because it is quite unsafe to accept the established date of the erection of a house as necessarily the date of its entrance, it is difficult to say what particular design of ornamental doorway was first used. Also, practically all of the old city houses, where ornamental designs were doubtless first and most generally used, have disappeared, leaving no clew to the pattern of their entrances. Accepting the asserted dates of their erection, and assuming that the doorways are the originals, the design sometimes called the "swan's-neck" appears among the earliest. It shows on the Parson Williams house, in Deerfield (date given as 1707); on the Porter house, in Hadley (given as 1713); on the long since destroyed Clark-Frankland house, in Boston (given as 1713); and a few other ancient structures. The earliest type, of course, was a mere flat boarding, or casing, at the sides and top of the opening. In many of the seventeenth-century buildings, anything more than this was not possible. In one-story houses, the top of the entrance was only a few inches below the eaves, and in many two-story houses the lintel was just below the overhang of the second story. As the use of the overhang was common in the seventeenth century, we must assume that the ornamental doorway was quite infrequent in that period. There are, however, houses of that time with more or less elaborate doorways. In not a few cases it is found that, at some later time and perhaps to make an ornamental doorway possible, the face line of the projecting second story has been carried down to the ground, thus giving a uniform surface to the whole front. This was done, for instance, on the House of Seven Gables, in Salem. The practice, probably not at all uncommon, often accounts for an apparent discrepancy between the age of a house and the design of its doorway.

But, after all, few of us care very much about the architectural technicalities of these charming relics of the days of our ancestors. We are told that this house or that has "chamfered beams," and we must go to a specialist or to the dictionary to find the meaning of the term. We are told that the early New England architecture perpetuates the "half-timber" method of house construction common enough in old England. But most of us care little and know less about that. Our interest lies far more in the picturesque or the historical features. Regarded as ornamental doorways only, most of us doubtless find more interest in the elaborate and graceful porched entrances of the later Georgian period than we do in the simpler types of the early Georgian, a difference illustrated, perhaps, by Salem or Portsmouth as compared with such places as Warren, Wickford, or Guilford. Both groups have their own particular charm, but the latter greatly exceed the former both in number and in variety of design.

It is a fair inference that people built houses with ornamental doorways, or added such doorways to houses already built, because it was fashionable; because their neighbors had them. This is clearly indicated, in a number of areas, by the use of the same or similar designs on houses of different ages. In his *Essay on Building*, Lord Bacon declared that "Houses are built to live in, and not to look on." This view appears to have been endorsed, generally, by the Americans of the seventeenth century. Their houses were of simple, rectangular lines. Their doorways were mere openings, arranged

for convenience, and without embellishment. They
were openings affording passage through outside or
inside walls. This was not because all were poor,
and could afford no decoration. Many were quite
well-to-do. It was the custom of the place and time.
Simplicity was the fashion in garb and in house.
This prevailed for nearly a hundred years, although
there was a gradual lessening of its force, more particularly in the matter of apparel. But, in the early
years of the eighteenth century, the Baconian idea
was somewhat disputed. A certain attention was
paid to the house from the standpoint of those who
might "look on" it. The decoration of house-fronts
by means of an ornamental doorway became steadily
a common practice. The simple rectangle of the
building itself persisted and the decorative doorway
really served to enhance the charming simplicity
of the structure. A little later, this extended to
a simple but effective decoration above the window-
openings, and, still later, to somewhat elaborate
and ornate cornices. An occasional oddity appeared,
as in the case of the House of Seven Gables, but for
nearly two hundred years the New England fashion
in houses was the simple type of rectangular building with doorway, window-opening, and cornice

[14]

decoration, sometimes singly and sometimes in combination. The city "mansions" of the later Georgian period differed from their predecessors only
in size and elaborateness of portal and other decoration.

So many old houses have disappeared leaving
behind them no plans, no working drawings, and
no pictures, that it is difficult if not impossible to
fix with any exactness the beginning of what may
be called the "porch period." There are many old
houses with a porch projecting from above the doorway. Many of these are a part of the original structure; probably most of them are. But many are
of a date long after that of the building of the house.
The two sections of New England in which may be
found the greatest number of old houses and old
doorways are, broadly, eastern Massachusetts and
western Connecticut. These were the fields of the
largest of the early settlements. I have made no
count of the individual cases, but my impression,
amounting almost to a conviction, is that the porch
is common in Connecticut and unusual in Massachusetts. This is in reference to old and not to modern houses. At some undetermined time, the Massachusetts area adopted the recessed doorway, some-

what unusual in the Connecticut area, and serving the purpose of the porch, namely, shelter for one who might have to wait for entrance. Before the use of these devices, the user of the doorway, on a rainy day, was obliged to stand in the dripping from the roof, not in early days provided with metal gutters nor, in many cases, even with a wooden trough. The porch and the recessed door also afforded their measure of protection from the rays of a hot summer sun. The physical reason for their construction is obvious, but we may assume that they were also regarded as ornamental.

In not infrequent cases, a porch appears hiding, largely, an elaborate doorway. In most instances of that kind, we may infer that the sheltering porch is an addition of somewhat later date than the erection of the house, or of its adornment by an ornamental entrance. Most, though by no means all, of these porches are narrow, barely more than the width of the door itself. Frequently, where the door has side-lights, the porch includes them. These little projections afford an interest even aside from the doorways. All may seem quite alike to the careless observer, but their variations are many, almost endless. Many village houses built in the last half of the nineteenth century show a small canopy projecting above the entrance and supported by brackets instead of columns, but this device is not often found on the older houses. While other shapes are not unusual, the more common form was pyramidal, a small gable with pilasters on the house wall and columns at its outer end. The columns vary in design; round, square, fluted, with plain and with decorated capitals, with and without pedestals. In both the gable and the other designs, there is wide variety. The flat entablature runs all the way from the severely plain to the elaborate, with dentils and carved frieze. In the gable, or pyramidal, type the inner line or ceiling may follow the slope of the outer line, or it may be arched. Not infrequently, it is flat, the face of the pediment showing the conventional "tympanum." They frequently show some simple decoration, dentils or a device of the Grecian Doric order, or both. From such information as I have been able to gather from professional sources, it would appear that while porches were used to some extent prior to that time, the device did not come into any general use until the early years of the nineteenth century. The veranda, frequently miscalled the "piazza," is of a later date.

It is now regarded as an almost indispensable feature of a house in the country, whether large or small, but our forefathers got along without them for something like two hundred years.

The lights around the doors are another interesting study. The name given to the light above the door, "fan-light," because of its shape, like a lady's fan, would seem to indicate that as one of the earliest patterns used. In many of the older houses of one story, and in not a few of those of two stories, the door opened immediately into a room. In many, and in probably most, of the two-story buildings it opened into a little box of a hall, six feet or so square. A part of this was occupied by a narrow and steep stairway proceeding by angular turns to the floor above. The early custom of building a house around a middle chimney, with fireplaces in the rooms about it, prohibited the use of a central or spacious hallway. The fan-light was evidently adopted as a means of lighting, to some extent, the little box that served the double purpose of an entrance-hall and a place for a stairway. In the more modest structures, a row of small panes, usually rectangular, afforded the desired lighting. When in the form of a segment of a circle, the fan-light is often an ornamental design, of simple but graceful lines, the glass usually set in lead. Side-lights were much less commonly used than fan-lights. They range from panes of common glass, arranged vertically, to ornamental designs. Not infrequently, they appear in combination with fan-lights. A modern improvement in the lighting of these little hallways is found in the use of doors with glass panels instead of wood.

Salem is probably the most widely known and best advertised field for hunters of Old New England doorways, but Portsmouth is quite inclined to regard itself as, at least, a rival claimant for the honor of presenting the most and the best. These hold their pre-eminence mainly by reason of the portals of houses built after the Revolution, although some of the "mansion houses" of both were built prior to that event. But there are other centres, somewhat less well known, that are, in their way, quite as interesting as Salem or Portsmouth. There are a number of excellent examples in Providence, and there are many in the near neighborhood of that city. Somewhat to my surprise, Newport had little to offer. In earlier days, there must have been many in that city, notable as it has been for many years as a centre of wealth and fashion. The modern multi-millionaires who have built their costly palaces along the shore did not make the place. In the years immediately preceding the Revolution, Newport was a busy and highly prosperous commercial centre, with rich merchants who built for themselves houses that were more or less palatial in their day and time. Most of those buildings are now gone, and most of those that still remain show little sign of their earlier grandeur. But some of the towns in the vicinity of Newport are fruitful fields for doorway-hunters. Many excellent designs may be seen in Warren, Bristol, Wickford, and a few other places. Most of them, however, are of the simpler type, that is, pilasters with entablatures or pediments rather than the built-out porches with both pilasters and columns such as appear on many of the later Georgian mansions.

Most of the cities of New England occupy the ground on which stood the villages of the seventeenth and eighteenth centuries. The old village site is, in most of them, covered by modern structures of brick and stone and steel. Here and there stand a few old houses that, when they were built, were on the outskirts of the village. But, aside from such well-known fields as Salem and Portsmouth, the larger cities have little to show in the way of old-time doorways. The best centres, in my experience, are the towns and villages of early settlement. But even such places present the charm of uncertainty. There are old towns with old-time houses but with few or no interesting doorways. From various excursions, my conclusion is that the Connecticut valley from the Sound to the Vermont line is, on the whole, the most fruitful area. Inasmuch, however, as that field covers approximately four thousand square miles, the difficulty of covering it exhaustively is obvious. The northeastern quarter of Massachusetts, with excursions across the border into southern New Hampshire, is another good hunting-ground. So, also, is little Rhode Island, which Doctor Holmes declared to be "a small but delightful State in the neighborhood of Pawtucket."

But the pleasure of hunting for old doorways in New England lies almost as much in the search as in the discovery.

PLATES

Kittery, Maine

Portland, Maine

Fryeburg, Maine

Scarboro, Maine

Portsmouth, New Hampshire   Warner House, 1718.

Portsmouth, New Hampshire

Portsmouth, New Hampshire

Portsmouth, New Hampshire

Portsmouth, New Hampshire

Portsmouth, New Hampshire

Bedford, Massachusetts

Newbury, Massachusetts

Newburyport, Massachusetts

Newburyport, Massachusetts

Williamstown, Massachusetts

Arlington, Massachusetts

Lexington, Massachusetts

Shrewsbury, Massachusetts

East Windsor Hill, Connecticut

East Windsor Hill, Connecticut

New Canaan, Connecticut

Farmington, Connecticut

Farmington, Connecticut

Farmington, Connecticut

Hatfield, Massachusetts

North Woburn, Massachusetts

Litchfield, Connecticut

Litchfield, Connecticut

Middlebury, Connecticut

East Windsor Hill, Connecticut

Wethersfield, Connecticut

Middletown, Connecticut

Guilford, Connecticut

Guilford, Connecticut

Newport, Rhode Island

Rocky Hill, Connecticut

Southington, Connecticut

Southbury, Connecticut

Southbury, Connecticut

New Haven, Connecticut

New Haven, Connecticut

Winsted, Connecticut

Deerfield, Massachusetts

Deerfield, Massachusetts

Deerfield, Massachusetts

Deerfield, Massachusetts

Deerfield, Massachusetts

Billerica, Massachusetts

Hadley, Massachusetts

Hadley, Massachusetts

Byfield, Massachusetts   Governor Dummer Mansion, about 1715.

Salem, Massachusetts   Nathan Robinson House, 1804.

Salem, Massachusetts Dodge - Shreves House, 1816

Salem, Massachusetts

Salem, Massachusetts

Deerfield, Massachusetts

Deerfield, Massachusetts

Deerfield, Massachusetts

Portsmouth, New Hampshire

North Hartland, Vermont

Bristol, Rhode Island

Warren, Rhode Island

Warren, Rhode Island

Warren, Rhode Island

Warren, Rhode Island

Wickford, Rhode Island